by A.J. Iguchi
illustrated by Rex Barron

SCHOOL PUBLISHERS

Printed in China

ISBN 10:   0-15-377363-4
ISBN 13:   978-0-15-377363-1

Ordering Options
ISBN 10:   0-15-377148-8 (Grade 4 Collection)
ISBN 13:   978-0-15-377148-4 (Grade 4 Collection)
ISBN 10:   0-15-377850-4 (package of 5)
ISBN 13:   978-0-15-377850-6 (package of 5)

2 3 4 5 6 7 8 9 10 0940 17 16 15 14 13 12 11 10 09

It was a beautiful spring evening in Miami, Florida. Velesta and her friend Marta were patiently waiting in Velesta's backyard. Marta had a glass jar ready to go. The sky darkened, and a few minutes later, fireflies began to appear. Their green-yellow lights flashed on and off throughout the yard.

"There's one back there!" yelled Velesta. The girls hurried toward the garage, and a moment later, a firefly lit up. Marta quickly cupped the bug in her hands while Velesta unscrewed the lid from the jar. Then Marta placed the firefly inside and said, "She is the most beautiful firefly I have ever seen!"

"I know," said Velesta, setting the jar on the patio table. "We are so lucky we caught her. Let's leave her out here, and we'll check on her tomorrow night."

Fiona the firefly looked out into the yard. All the other fireflies were gone now. She suddenly felt very alone. She tried her best to squeeze out of the jar, but it was impossible. She became nervous and began to fidget. "I'll never get out of here," she thought forlornly, staring out into the dark yard.

A moment later, she heard a rumbling noise. It was Raymond the raccoon, scrounging around for food. Raymond lived in one of the trees in the yard.

"Raymond, please help me!" yelled Fiona from inside the jar. Raymond turned his head, walked over, and looked at Fiona.

"I think I can get you out of there, friend," said Raymond. "Unlike you fireflies, we raccoons have nice little paws that work almost as well as hands." Raymond smiled and held up his paws for Fiona to admire.

"That's great, but can you please start *using* them?" asked Fiona. Raymond nodded and got right down to business. He stood on his back legs, held the jar against his body, and tried with all his might to twist off the cap with his paws. The cap would not budge.

"Unfortunately, these fine little paws are just *too* little," said Raymond. "However, I have another idea."

Raymond walked into the back part of the yard where there were bushes and trees. He found Steven, the snake, curled up under a bush. Steven eyed Raymond suspiciously, especially since raccoons don't mind eating snakes on occasion.

"Don't worry, Steven, I'm not hungry," said Raymond, as Steven stayed hidden under the bush.

"Then what can I do for you?" asked the snake.

"I wonder if you could help my friend," said Raymond hopefully.

"Will your friend try to eat me?" asked Steven, still not moving.

"A firefly eat a snake? Not on this planet! Come on, you'll be fine," said Raymond as Steven slowly slithered out and followed him.

"My paws are too small to grip the cap, but you just might be able to wrap yourself around it and unscrew it," Raymond explained.

"I'll certainly give it a try," said Steven. He stretched out his tail and wrapped it around the top of the patio chair. Then he curled the rest of his body around the jar cap and tried to unscrew it.

"Wrong way––you're tightening it," said Raymond.

"Oh, right, I always mess that up," said Steven. He tried to turn the cap the other way, but it was no use: the cap would simply not come off.

"Thanks anyway, Steven," said Fiona sadly as Steven slithered away.

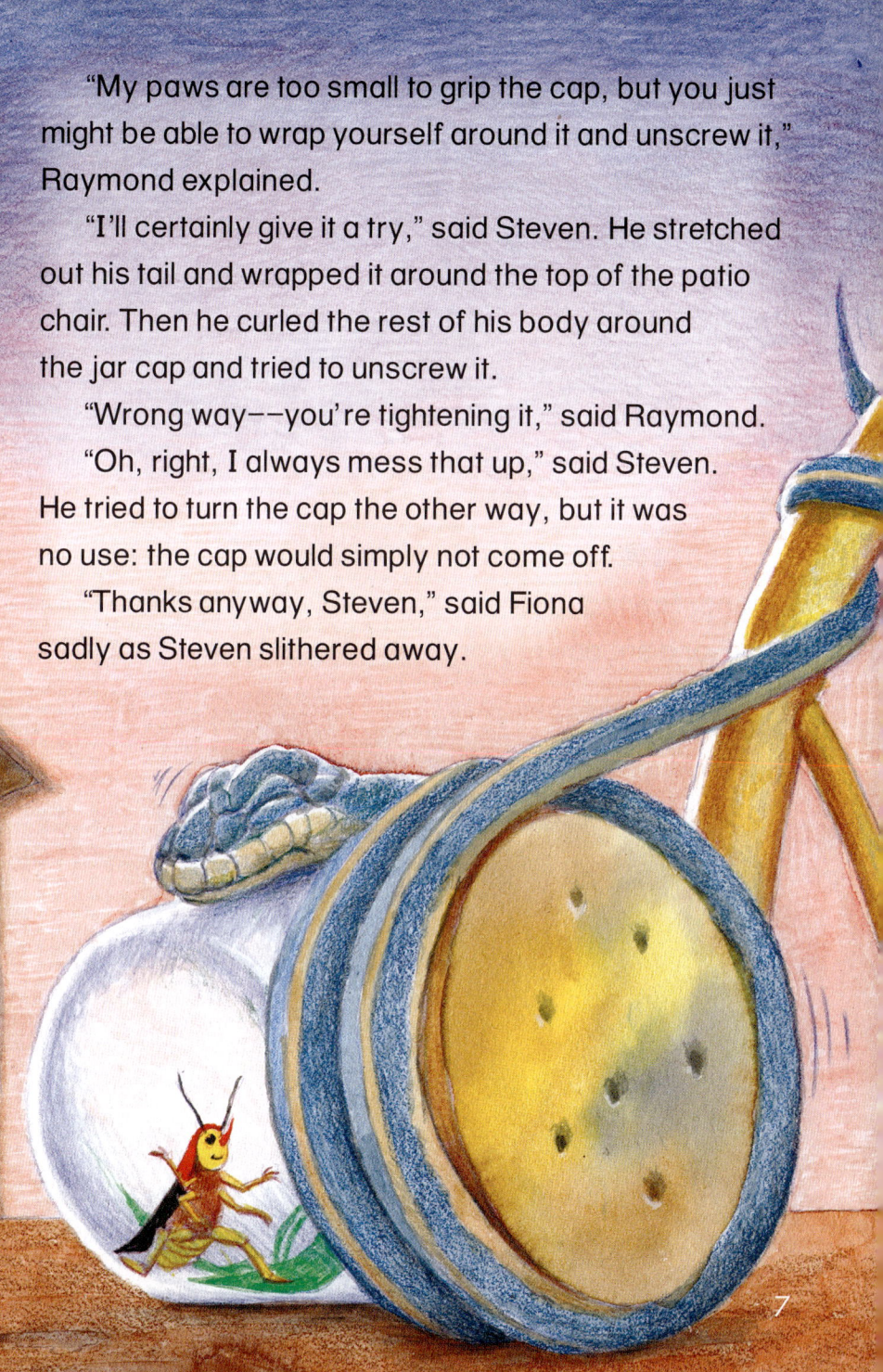

"I'm never going to get out of here! Tomorrow night the girls will come back to give me some food, and then they'll put the cap right back on the jar!" cried Fiona.

"Listen, Fiona, I'll get you out of that jar one way or another," said Raymond. "Tomorrow, during the day, I'm going to find a way."

"You're nocturnal, so you sleep during the day. How will you be able to help me?" asked Fiona.

"Oh, I can give up a few hours of sleep to help a friend," said Raymond.

"That's very noble of you, Raymond," replied Fiona, smiling. Raymond walked away to find some food, and Fiona sat down, wondering if she'd ever escape.

The next morning when Fiona woke up, she saw Raymond hurrying over to the patio. There were fifteen white seagulls flying right behind him.

"Good morning, Fiona, and please say hello to my friends from the coast," said Raymond.

"Hi," Fiona said, as the birds perched on the table. Raymond nodded to the birds, and they immediately started to take turns pecking at the top of the lid.

"They have strong beaks, so they just might be able to pry that lid off," explained Raymond. After several minutes, it became apparent that the lid wasn't going to budge.

"Come on, guys—I saw an open picnic basket at the beach when we were flying over here," said Cliff, the leader of the seagulls. The flock flew off.

 While Raymond was reassuring his friend Fiona that
he would resolve the issue, he noticed a long line of
ants marching through the yard. His eyes immediately lit
up with an idea. Within minutes, Raymond had fifty ants
on the table, listening to his plan.

 "I know you ants have incredible strength. I've
even heard you can carry objects heavier than your
own body weight. Surely you can pull this lid off," said
Raymond. The ants crawled up the jar and tried their
hardest to force the lid off the jar. As usual, though,
the lid stayed put.

Raymond left to take a nap, but he returned in the evening when the girls came to check on Fiona. He hid in the bushes while the girls gave Fiona some grass. Then Raymond noticed Benny the bat swoop into the yard in pursuit of a mosquito. When the girls left, Raymond called Benny over for a chat.

"You're asking me to unscrew a lid? That's kind of a pathetic idea, Ray, since I don't really have hands," said Benny. "You obviously need a better plan."

"Do you have something in mind?" asked Fiona.

"Of course," said Benny proudly.

11

"So what's the plan, Benny?" asked Raymond.

"Easy now, Raymond—you haven't even told me what I get for helping out," said Benny.

"Why can't you just help out because it's the right thing to do?" asked Fiona.

"Because I'm a stingy guy, and no one gets anything for free from Benny," replied Benny. Fiona and Raymond looked at each other.

"How about if I show you the best fruit tree in the neighborhood? You can go there and eat all you want," said Raymond.

"That's a definite deal," said Benny.

The next evening, Velesta and Marta came out to feed Fiona. When the girls went back inside the house, Raymond told Fiona that Benny the bat had a last-ditch plan to free her from the jar.

"Wrap yourself up in a leaf and cover your eyes, Fiona," Raymond said.

With that, Benny swooped into the yard and smashed right into Fiona's jar! The jar crashed to the ground and broke wide open. Fiona dusted herself off and looked around. She was free at last! She carefully crawled out of the jar and hurried back to the tree where Raymond slept.

When Fiona arrived at the tree, Benny was contentedly hanging upside down from a tree branch, looking very pleased with himself. "Your plan worked perfectly, Benny!" said Fiona happily.

"Hey, I know what I'm doing, kid," said Benny, and a moment later Raymond crawled into the tree.

"Raymond, thank you *so much*," said Fiona.

"That's what friends are for," said Raymond, smiling a big raccoon grin.

Think Critically

1. What animals tried to free Fiona? List them in order from first to last.

2. What did Raymond have to do to get Benny's help?

3. How would you describe Raymond?

4. What word means almost the same thing as *stingy* does on page 12?

5. What did you find most amusing in this story? Why?

 **Math**

Find the Sum Say there are 150 fireflies in Velesta's backyard every night. Write a math problem to figure out what the total number of fireflies would be for the month of July. Solve your math problem.

School-Home Connection Discuss this book with a family member. Then have a discussion about the things that good friends do for one another.